CALL ME HERO

FOR MY HERO, DAVID- CBB
To my Mom, Kay Beard Williams, dog lover extraordinaire- KWG
www.clairebatemanbooks.com

SPECIAL THANKS

Amelia Marchand, Julie Hoffman, Nolde Alexius, Rachel Hadley, Sue Chenevert,
Sarah Kracke, Tricia Berryman, Lisa Steen Proctor, Jady Regard, Scott Henry,
Julie Wartell, Mary Anne Smith, Carolyn Murphy's 4th Grade Class, Lucille Harold,
Bob & Lucy Smith, Jerry Smith, Damian and Douglas Boudreaux, Alyce-Elise Hoge,
Alan Graham, Anne Pancol, Renee Bacher, Drew Bateman, Susan Marchand,
The medical team under I-10 at Old Metairie Road, Rick Compeaux, Barry Kelley,
Nancy Jo Craig, Kip Holden, Brady Patin, St. Aloysius School and Church, the volunteers
of Mobile Loaves & Fishes, Ricky Hartford, Ginger Guttner and Frankie Gould

Shell Beach Publishing, 6010 Perkins Road, Suite A, Baton Rouge, Louisiana 70808. Copyright © 2008 by Claire
Boudreaux Bateman. All Rights Reserved. No part of this publication may be reproduced, or stored in a retrieval
system or transmitted in any form or by any means, electronic, mechanical, photocopying, recording, or otherwise,
without written permission of the publisher. Art Direction by Chris Steiner. Digital Photography by David Humphreys. Printed in China. ISBN 978-0-9706732-4-4. First Edition

CALL ME HERO

Written by Claire Boudreaux Bateman
illustrated by Kym W. Garraway

The New Orleans sky was not yet black. Afternoon sounds of Hutch and his neighborhood friends faded as the dinner bell rang. I made my way down the front steps of our home. I could smell barbeque at the Palmer's house.

Across the street, on a porch swing, sat a young couple with their new baby. "Hey there, Hero," the man called out with a smile. "You looking for trouble tonight?"

"The man knows a hero when he sees one," I thought to myself, striking out on my evening prowl. The sky was beginning to sprinkle.

I got a whiff of the moon vine in old Mr. Whitaker's yard. I loved chasing his cat through the flower garden, but I knew better. Mr. Whitaker told Hutch if he ever caught me in his yard again he'd send me to the pound.

In the rain, I walked my normal nighttime beat to the neighborhood market. The weather was keeping away the regulars at all my hot spots. There were no scraps at the pizza joint and the grocery store stock boys were nowhere in sight. On my way home, water was so deep in some places, I even had to swim. I passed by Mr. Whitaker's house again and noticed his windows were covered with boards. "Hmmm," I thought, "maybe he's gone. Here's my chance to get that cat!"

"Hero! Come on boy!" Hutch was calling me. What was he doing awake in the middle of the night? Whatever he wanted would have to wait.

I slipped through Whitaker's fence, wiggled past the bushes and sniffed around for the cat. I wasn't on the porch long when I noticed the water covering my paws. I realized I'd better hurry home. I would have to swim.

The current carried me for blocks. As I floated past my house, I knew Hutch was gone.

THE CITY WAS DISAPPEARING UNDER THE WATER.

I dug my claws into a tree limb and pulled myself out of the rising tide. I don't know how long I stayed there, but when the rain finally stopped, the sun shone down hard. Every step mattered as I carefully crept along fallen telephone poles to the roof of a nearby house. I heard voices inside.

I waited on the roof for two long, hot days before I saw the man in his boat.

"You okay, boy?" the man asked, coming up on me slowly. He was holding a bottle of water. I knew it was for me.

Weak from waiting, I managed a meager bark.

"Are there people in this house, boy?"

I lapped up the water and barked again. The man broke a hole in the roof with his axe. Tired and thirsty, the people came out one by one and thanked him for rescuing them.

"Don't thank me," the man said. "If it weren't for your dog, I never would have heard you in there."

"That's not our dog," the people answered.

"Well, then," the man said looking at me, "it looks like I have a side kick, doesn't it? I'll bring him home with me to Baton Rouge and we'll try to find his owner."

THE MOMENT MY PAWS HIT THE GROUND, I HEARD CHILDREN.

"Mom," they announced, "Daddy's back! Daddy, you made it home!"

Listening to the voices of the man's children made my tired tail wag.

The boy was the first one to see me. "Oh. My. Gosh," he said. "Dad, did you save this dog from Hurricane Katrina?"

The man smiled. "Yes, I saved him. But this dog is the real hero."

"What's his name, Dad?" the boy asked. He was stroking my back. It felt so good.

"My name is Hero," I thought. "You heard the man! Call me Hero!"

I listened as he told his family how we met.

"This little dog led us around the flooded city of New Orleans all day," the man said. "Every time he barked at a house, there were people trapped inside. Rescue groups from around the country followed our boat to see where he would lead us next. He must have found over 50 people today."

"HE SOUNDS LIKE A REAL NEW ORLEANS SAINT, DAD," SAID THE LITTLE BOY.

"A saint, huh?" the man said, scratching his chin. "Son, do you know how to say 'saint' in Spanish?"

"Santos," the boy answered proudly.

The man smiled at me and said, "Come on Santos, let's get you something to eat."

My legs were heavy as I followed the man through the kitchen where women were cutting up chicken and sausage. Children stood on either side of the dining room table making sandwiches. Outside a man was cooking over large pots. Something smelled delicious.

I filled my belly with warm
jambalaya and fell fast asleep to
the sound of people talking.

The next day the man and his son took me to LSU to find my family.

"Okay, Santos, here's your chance," the boy said. "All of these buses are full of people from New Orleans. You just let us know if you recognize anyone."

I recognized someone, all right. It was old Mr. Whitaker! He was in a wheelchair. Loud helicopters were landing nearby. I was able to sneak past him without being noticed. If he saw me here without Hutch, he'd send me to the pound for sure.

Inside, the boy led me through cots and lines of doctors and nurses. Volunteers were handing out blankets, clothes, shoes, food, you name it. I thought only of Hutch. If Mr. Whitaker was here, surely Hutch would be, too.

"LOOK DAD," THE BOY SAID. HE WAS POINTING TO A WOMAN SURROUNDED BY PHONES AND COMPUTERS.

"Excuse me, ma'am," the man said. "We're looking for this little guy's owner. He was quite a hero when we found him in New Orleans the other day."

Impressed by the story, the woman asked, "What's his name?"

"Hero," I thought, standing tall. "Didn't you hear the man? My name is Hero."

The boy was rubbing my ears. "There were no tags on his collar," he told her.

"Hmmm. That makes it difficult," the woman said. "But we can put his description in this database with your name and number. Maybe his owner will recognize him and call you. Busloads of people are arriving here about every twenty minutes. But these are the people who need doctors," she explained. "Once they are feeling better they'll go downtown to the River Center. You may want to check there in a couple of days."

"Rise and shine fellas," the man called to the boy and me. "We've got food to deliver. Folks from Austin, Texas are meeting us at the interstate."

The boy was out of the bed faster than I was. It was still dark outside as I watched him and his dad load ice chests of sandwiches and jambalaya into the back of their pickup.

In the early morning light, we saw the big truck from Austin. A group of volunteers jumped out and began transferring the ice chests from our truck to theirs. "We have our route ready for the Mississippi Gulf Coast," the driver said.

"How's it looking in Mississippi?" the man asked.

"It was hit hard. Entire towns are gone," the driver answered. "Church groups have set up all through the region and are waiting to help us deliver this food. We can't thank you enough for preparing everything."

"Don't mention it," the man said.

On our way back to the man's house, the boy asked, "How long will we keep making food, Dad?"

"It's not just the people who have been hurt by the storm who need to be fed, son," the man explained. "People from all over the United States have come here to help us with the rescue work. When you go to school tomorrow you'll see that the playground is full of tents. The men and women sleeping in those tents are working in New Orleans during the day. At night, families from your school are feeding them. Tonight, they will eat our jambalaya."

"That's good news for Santos, too." the boy said, scratching me behind my ears. "He loves the scraps!"

DAYS PASSED, AND STILL WE HEARD NOTHING FROM HUTCH. IN THE AFTERNOONS, I WAITED FOR THE BOY AT THE BUS STOP.

"Santos!" he would cry. He was always so happy to see me, but that name was all wrong. One day the boy stepped down from the bus and said, "Today, we're going to the River Center to look for your owner."

We arrived and parked in the loading dock. I followed behind the man and the boy. We passed high piles of clothes, diapers, food, shoes, and toys for children. There were people signing up to be trained as volunteers, people serving food, people with radios, and many, many people who were displaced by the hurricane.

I saw a group of boys playing soccer. "Could that be Hutch?" I began to run.

"NO DOGS ALLOWED IN HERE!" A GUARD GROWLED. MY HEART WAS POUNDING, BUT I KEPT THE BOYS IN MY SIGHT.

"This dog was rescued after the storm," the man told the guard. "We are here to find his owner."

"Does he have a name?" the guard asked.

"Yes, of course I have a name! My name is Hero!" I thought. The soccer game was moving in our direction. I looked at the face of each player. None of them was Hutch.

"Dogs are being taken to the shelter at LSU," the guard said. "If you want, you can drop him off there."

My attention was back on the guard. "Drop me off? WHAT?" I thought, barking loudly.

"My neighbor volunteers there," the man said to the guard. "I'll ask her to post his photograph."

"What's a shelter, Dad?" the boy asked after we climbed back in the truck. "A shelter is where you go when you don't have a home anymore," the man said. "There are shelters all over the state. Some are for dogs and some are for people," he explained.

"I HEARD AT ONE ANIMAL SHELTER THEY RING A BIG BELL EVERY TIME AN OWNER IS REUNITED WITH THEIR PET."

I closed my eyes and tried to imagine that bell ringing for me. Surely Hutch missed me. He missed me in the middle of his soccer game and surely he missed the birds and other animals I'd bring to his door. I was a good dog, wasn't I? He let me sleep in his room. I could see Hutch in my mind. I could hear his voice. Then I thought of the last time I was called Hero. It was the night of the storm. Instead of going after Mr. Whitaker's cat, I should have gone home.

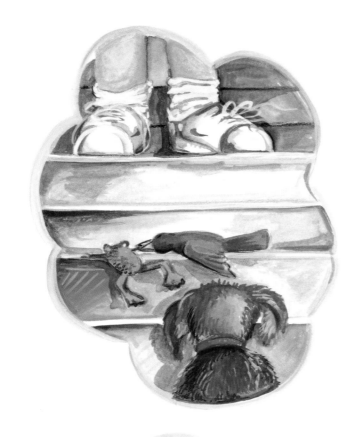

The man interrupted my thoughts. "Maybe Santos' owner is in Shreveport," he said. "Your uncle is working at a people shelter there. I'll ask him to hang a picture of Santos. How about that?" the man asked. "I'll bet there are a lot of people there."

THE TRUCK WAS QUIET FOR A MOMENT. MY HEART WAS HEAVY WITH MEMORIES OF HUTCH AND MY FAMILY IN NEW ORLEANS.

"Maybe you're right, Dad," the boy said. He pulled me close into his chest and gave me a squeeze. "Maybe his owner is in Shreveport."

THE YARD WAS FULL OF NEIGHBORHOOD BOYS. "CATCH IT, SANTOS!" THEY YELLED.

Frisbee football was one of my new favorite games. There was always a fight about who would add me to their team. Our afternoon game was growing. "These are my cousins from Texas," I heard one kid say. "They're staying with us because of the new hurricane."

"There is another hurricane," the boy explained. "This one is supposed to be as big as Katrina," he said as we walked to the house. Inside, the living room was full of new faces. The television held everyone's attention. "Hurricane Rita is destroying the Gulf Coast between Texas and Louisiana," the reporter announced.

The next day, I heard a woman crying. Her home in Cameron, Louisiana had been destroyed by Hurricane Rita.

"I'm off of work all next week," the man said. He was trying to console her. "We will go to Cameron to help clean up."

"Can we bring Santos, Dad?" the boy asked.

"I wouldn't go without him," the man assured him.

The city of Cameron was under water. We rode in boats
looking for blocked drainage canals. I jumped in the water.
When the current pulled me toward the holes, the volunteers,
who came from all across the country, knew where to do their
work. Once the holes were cleared the water could flow out
of the town. It was like draining a giant bathtub.

DEBRIS FROM THE STORM
NEEDED TO BE CLEARED FROM
THE ROADWAYS. THE RESCUE
WORKERS USED CHAINSAWS
TO CUT THROUGH FALLEN TREES
WHILE THE BOY AND I WATCHED.

But suddenly, I sensed danger nearby and barked loudly. I looked all around me and discovered a large snake near the boy's leg. The man thought the sound of the chainsaws had frightened me and tried to calm me down.

"It's okay Santos. This won't take long," he said.

I barked louder and louder, never taking my eyes off of the snake. Finally, the man saw it near the boy's leg and quickly lifted his son out of harm's way.

"Good boy, Santos," he said, patting me on the head. Then he looked at his son. "You and Santos get in the truck and keep a lookout for more snakes while we finish clearing this road."

PEOPLE AND PETS WEREN'T THE ONLY ONES WHO HAD LOST THEIR HOMES. WE FOUND COWS TRAPPED ON LEVEES.

During the storm, they had walked to the high ridges of land to keep from drowning. Now, water separated them from their pastures. They were hungry and thirsty. The rescue workers herded the cattle on horseback as I swam out in front, leading the way to dry pastureland.

We spent a week in Cameron. Each night, I curled up next to the boy. Other than the occasional marsh mosquito, the only sound I heard was the soothing rhythm of his breathing. It rocked me to sleep.

"Load 'em up," the man called to the boy and me. "It's time to go home."

"Dad, that was awesome," the boy said. "Can we head over to Texas, and see if they need us, too?"

The man smiled at his son. "It feels good to help people, doesn't it?" he asked. "I'm very proud of you and how hard you worked," he said. "And I'm proud of Santos."

"What? The man is proud of ME?" I thought.

"I know, Dad," the boy said. "Santos saved me from that snake and he swam in that scary water and led the cattle back. Everyone loved him. I wish we could keep him."

"HE'S NOT JUST A SAINT, DAD, HE'S A HERO."

It felt good to hear the boy call me "Hero." But I liked the other part, too…the part about keeping me."

"Well fella, what do you say?" the man asked. "Will you stay and be our Santos?"

"You bet I'll stay!" I was wagging my tail, "And Santos is fine with me," I thought. "There are too many heroes around here anyway!"

MY HERO STORY

WRITTEN BY:

ABOUT THE STORY

Three days after Hurricane Katrina devastated the coastlines of Louisiana and Mississippi, a group of men calling themselves "The Cajun Coast Guard" arranged a rendezvous on Interstate 10 and trailered their boats to the flooded city of New Orleans. I'll never forget watching all of those trucks pulling all of those boats. There were hundreds of them. The news was reporting rumors of drug addicts, looters and pyromaniacs. My husband, David, was driving one of those trucks and I was scared to see him head into a dangerous situation, but I knew I couldn't stop him. My heart swells with pride when I think of him pulling people from hot attics, bringing helpless animals to safety, or encouraging people to shimmy down their roofs into his boat. One of our friends, Jonathan Rice, was there, too. Jonathan found a dog he just couldn't leave in New Orleans; a fragile German Shepherd with no collar. While Jonathan nursed him back to health and searched for the dog's owner, he called him Santos...and still does. Jonathan and David aren't doctors or nurses; they aren't fire fighters or policemen. On a regular day, they are lawyers. But on that day, they were heroes.

The man and boy in this story represent all of the many *nameless* heroes who helped restore this region after Hurricanes Katrina and Rita. This book is for them.

CALLING ALL HEROES

Water wasn't the only thing flooding the streets of New Orleans after Hurricane Katrina. There was also a flood of kindness and compassion from non-profits, grassroots organizations and church groups. Ten percent of the cost of each book will be donated to non-profits doing disaster relief work, not just in this area but wherever there is a need. Please visit my website, www.callmehero.com, where you can send me both your hero story and the name of your favorite non-profit organization.

To all of you heroes out there-
Merci Beaucoup,
Claire Bateman